Pieces Of Me

A POETIC COLLECTION

Emmanuel Netu

Order this book online at www.trafford.com
or email orders@trafford.com

Most Trafford titles are also available at major online book retailers.

Printed in the United States of America.

ISBN: 978-1-4269-6908-9 (sc)
ISBN: 978-1-4269-6909-6 (e)

Trafford rev. 05/09/2011

 www.trafford.com

North America & International
toll-free: 1 888 232 4444 (USA & Canada)
phone: 250 383 6864 ♦ fax: 812 355 4082

Pieces Of Me

Before we begin…

A short note of appreciation and gratitude for making this dream a reality.

Editors

Marlene Bakmazian

Monique Gruber

General Editor

Phil Dzidah

Publisher

Trafford Publishing

Forward...

What is "love"? Is it necessarily a feeling, a biological reaction or both? – For all I know it might be something else entirely. Now more than ever I feel that four letters have completely changed my life, as I'm sure they've changed yours. Hence, I've decided to pursue temporary madness and took it upon myself to express these overwhelming emotions to the best of my ability through my individual, filtered love experiences and sometimes "unrealistic" expectations.

Each piece is different for every single reader- And that, of course, means there's really no such thing as the "best poem". However there are and always have been favourite poems. The words you'll find within these pages express pieces of my love life and thoughts on romance.
I hope they'll be your favourite too…

Let the countdown begin.

-Netu -

A beautiful woman Part II

The greatest treasures are those invisible to the eyes
beautiful as you are,
know that it is your soul that captures me
your mind that masters power that holds me.
Evermore you take my breath away
Bringing forth a thousand joys with a touch and a kiss.
Stay for a while,
You are much more than curves and a smile
Yet here am I aroused by your glorious symmetry
Slowly caressing my mind as I will never forget your imagery
Your lips and hips.
But this only the outer shell of what is truly a delightful soul,
A beautiful mind and a true woman.

Hence as others be fooled by what only eyes can scout,
I remain enamoured by what emanates from the inside out.

-Netu-

Free at last

You are so beautiful you pass as freedom
liberating my fears and insecurities
With each breath you take, you are
fatal as you are, blissful, divine and always mine.
Oh so precious product of loveliness.
Your voice enchants me and your
eyes pierce through my soul
as if barriers never were-
Rest assured you are mine and I am
yours always.

-Netu-

Bound to you

Unsure that I should trust I've opened up
My heart buried deep
inside where you are.
And for the first time in my life
There is no need for freedom
You see,
There is so much that I've faced on my own or
Walls I built up became my home
But all is different now-There is you.
Sweetheart,
You take my breath away
With each beat you make;
The most soothing of melodies,
That bounds me to all that you are.

-Netu-

Easy

I should of known you we're trouble from the first kiss,
Felt like bliss, but now my eyes won't open.
I gave you all I had
And you toss it somewhere between
Forgotten memories and fairytales.
Regardless of the outcome
I can't control how I feel.
However,
It makes no sense for me to go through this pain
Because I'd never want you to feel the same.
You see, I thought you loved me,
But its clear that we actually never we're.
You mad yet oh so beautiful woman,
A perfect stranger you are,
Here today gone today
Yet all that remains is a name.

-Netu-

Call it what you will

I write this note to you in hopes that you
understand exactly what it is that you've done to me.
As of today you've taken every inch
of my love and changed what I used to be.
Call it what you will; love, lust or even temporary madness
But I am glad to be mad and
foolish for someone who understands me
who doesn't question my way of being, living breathing
and accepts me for who I am… just a man.
You have done to me what seems to be irreversible.
You beautiful woman nothing could amount to the emotion
I feel every time I hear your name,
You fine sweet thing
You've bewitched me
and I am oh so thankful.

-Netu-

As if words weren't enough

As if words weren't enough,
I'm here thinking about how much time has gone to waste,
All because of the misconception of love lust and all that's
    sweet below the waist.
I wish you could understand how you make me weak,
Never have I felt the need to breath slowly.
Here's hoping this message is not misunderstood,
I ask for nothing but find the need to inform you that
everything you do is devastating seductive and irresistible- Fatal
You are more than that, far above what the human mind can
    fathom as beautiful.
Whatever it is that you do, you do it well and however it is
    that you do it,
keep at it because it is the best feeling in the world to be
    loved by you.
Words aren't enough to describe how you've changed my
    perception on life-love,
and everything else that involves living breathing and being.
Best wishes to you wherever you may be,
because at this point in time,
this is but wishful thinking.

-Netu-

Timeless memories

Darling,

Good morning, good afternoon and goodnight to you; three phrases that I would like you to know that I think about whispering, yelling, saying each and every day especially for you. More so I wish to gaze at your face, touch your smooth skin and kiss your sweet lips forever. You are above and beyond all I've ever felt. I need you, want you and feel you through each inch of my being and believe in you through each fiber of my soul. You are ever so precious to me; don't forget that you are beautiful and I never want you to change who you are, ever, not even for me.

I know I can be selfish, I know I can want more than I can handle at times.. but the truth and the fact of the matter remains that you bring out the best in me, and for that, I love you today, now, tomorrow and forever.

Thank you

Yours truly...

-Netu-

Note to self

Listen, I don't want you to think I'm some sort of lunatic, some crazy individual that can't get past the fact that things are where they are-that's life. I get that, and I understand that I am where I am because of the decisions that I have made in my life, and had I made different ones previous to this moment, things may have been different. However, I must say this has been quite the journey; an experience of a life time. I have learned to appreciate what I never had before; love.

I am deeply and sincerely honoured to have met you regardless of what the outcome may be after you read this note. Here's hoping you understand my point of view and perhaps even consider reconsidering what it is that you're thinking of doing, but who am I to ask that of you? How dare I expect all of these things from you after I consciously did what I did. I don't have a reason to inspire reconsideration; I don't have anything to logically or emotionally explain what transpired before this letter. All I know is that what I feel wont leave me, and I've come to terms with that- I just hope you have.

Understand that I understand where I am in life, and am completely aware that things in life do not always turn out the way I want them to; that is clear and very understood. I would like for you to know that I also have done everything in my power to shake thoughts of you. Everything I could, I did, and yet the fact still remains that I love you. And regardless of the outcome of life, I do, and I always will. And that's that.

Now moving on to the reason why I'm writing this letter. This note is a release of my emotions, a way for me to get everything out in the open and never have to revisit it again. Hopefully getting this out of my system will either get you to see life through my eyes for a moment and or allow me to get thoughts, feelings, emotions out of my system, mind, body and free me from this... illusion; love.

I never understood why it was we met, I never questioned anything we did and although I regret not being able to respond in a manner that would secure a future between us, I am grateful for the times that we have spent, I am glad we've met I am happy you where in my life and are one of my best memories, the best memory of what it is and what it truly means to love and to fall in love; love.

Sincerely,

your soul mate

-Netu-

Back to you

May our tale be prolonged, my love.
For not quietly as of stupidity and fright did I
vary voice from faith's predictions.

poured forth are words from
my mouth,
imitating the speech of hope,
that I hold close to my heart.

O Queen, may you, with reason,
pursue the ambiguous path of this riddle.
Where fate will trace a way back to you.

-Netu-

Last words to love. – The pursuit of happiness

I've been told that
If you love set free,
If faith makes it so that its back
It's yours, otherwise, it never was.

So I had decided to take it slow,
saving up my love, my passion
ever so preciously for…

Before I knew it, all I asked for,
Became more and more overwhelming
It overtook my life my thoughts
My being and now I am consumed with
An ideal, a concept…

But I'm tired of crying and sick of bittersweet
Disappointments, expectations, let downs
over-promising and over delivering… and for what?
For who?— a concept of my ideal lover?

I guess the overtime drove me away,
Today I stand up
for everything that I chose to do for me.
I can say,
I'm turning around the life I let
an unrealistic conception of love siphon away.

I've decided, for my sake, to be loved for what I am,
And not for what I lend , or apparently desperately desire.
I pursue my own self, perusing and enjoying the fruits of my
Labour – A remedy for a soft kiss
I've vowed to end with bliss.

-When it comes, it will come, till then,
I live the pursuit of happiness.

-Netu-

Invisible essentials

I've been roaming around,
Feeling down, looking
at plenty of faces out of reach
Now more than ever I could use a miracle.
I'm talking about fate here – feelings
so powerful it's as if some force beyond
my control is guiding you beyond my
wildest dreams; like you.
Who's value is countless
You know that I could use somebody like you.
My emotions are waging wars
to shake off my heart's beats
Here's hoping you notice
That I've been roaming around,
Feeling like discovering that the bad things in life open
your eyes to the good things you
weren't paying attention to before.
As time passes by love becomes but
A word, used once to many times.
One can only see with the heart
Essentials are invisible to the eyes.
For what its worth,
The best portion of my life,
Will be the little, nameless, unremembered acts,
Of kindness to you. Grow old along with me,
the best is yet to be. Love is always bestowed as a gift –
freely, willingly, and without expectation....
I don't seek love to be loved; I love because
it is above and beyond me to
give something that I might never hope to find.

-Netu-

Toast to Alchemy

A word is no word until you say it A melody is no melody
    until you sing it
And love in your heart wasn't put there to stay
– because my love isn't love until you have it.
A good woman is hard to find
And a hard woman is good to find. So they tell me.

Here I stand softer than I should be,
Heart melted, alchemised from what I used to be
Our encounter brought out the best of me
And here's hoping our love can make
The rest of me. May I be your practical alchemy
The element in your life , highly sought-after.
Precious dense, soft, most malleable, ductile and pure.
May I serve as your symbol of wealth,

Cherish you with all of me, Thoughts, feelings, respect, gifts
Among which the most valuable is our love
Treat it as if it where gold, Ounce by ounce, beaten out
By series of unfortunate and fortunate events which I still
    ignore.

Finally, it will remain thin an unbreakable golden bond,
Hold it close and wrap it around your neck, lay it close to
    your heart, Where its suppose to be;
As a symbol of these words:

I will not lie, steal, cheat, or drink. But if must lie,
May it be in your arms. If I must steal, may it be to steal you
away from bad company. If I must cheat, may
I cheat our society's concept of true love
And be with you at your worst.
Finally, if I must drink, may I propose a toast to us,
Drink in the moments that take our breaths away and
Rejoice to the fact that " The meeting of our two personalities
Was like the contact of two chemical substances: a reaction,
That has forever transformed me in the best of ways."

-Netu-

I'll raise you

How dare they question me? Feeding your insecurities,
        telling you
that I don't know what love is and that I'm too young for this
        or that.
Poke-a-bluff, bet or raise them on my account,
take the best hand as they induce you to fold because you
have a better hold; on me.

Here's hoping that these words, these small words will give
        you bits and pieces of what
it is I feel, and what drives me to be so sure of myself when it
        comes to matters of the heart.
You see, I know I love because I have no choice, its above and
        beyond me,
I don't have to try to explain myself when I'm around you,
        being present
is a reason and an explanation in itself. It just is.

Its natural for me to hold you, to laugh at the perfect time
to understand the joke, or not but it'd never be awkward,
because we`re in sink, it just works between us don't you see
Folding immediately may decrease your chances of being hurt
In most cases, but this is a calculated risk.

A draw in which odds are strong enough for us
In this case, you are the exception,
even though life experience may have forced
others to fold their hands,
I'm all in.

-Netu-

Perfect stranger

So you stay there sitting on that chair, looking at me like you
    have no idea who I am,
if you knew how it makes me feel to know that you are
    exactly what I want
and yet you have no idea I am its torture I endure still.
I endure looking at you, gazing at what is in my mind the most
exceptional being on which I have every laid eyes.
Moments like this only happen once if at that in peoples` life
    times
yet here I am looking at you looking at me still asking myself
why I'm just looking. Why I have no driving force to make
    me say a word,
why this time love is paralyzing, why I feel like I cannot go
    forward.
It just kills me that all I know is your name,
perhaps that you like long walks, maybe that you
like to read from time to time and enjoy your coffee.
It kills me that your expressive, vibrant, intellectual,
that you know how to carry yourself and that I should
could, would but am still just looking.
Frustration is too weak of a word to express
how I feel, how you bring out all these emotions
and yet leave me motionless; gazing at you
like a perfect stranger.

-Netu-

I don't sparkle

You really want to know don't you?
Well… I'm not your regular type of guy,
I call often, I worry about you all the time,
I want to be with you as often as I possibly can,
I will stand with you come in the room,
I will sit after you do, I will open the door,
I enjoy long walks, I rather kiss… forever
I cuddle, I cuddle, I hug, I caress,
I think of more than I should,
I love to dance, with you, I will
Pin you against the wall every now and then
I will look at you even when your not saying a word,
I will take any reason and use every excuse in the book
To see you, touch you, be with you
I will not take no for an answer,
I enjoy long walks, passionate conversations
A great sense of humour a good story
I don't drink often; not at all, but if I do it will be with you
I dislike clubbing, I know every chick flick by heart,
I will debate about why I think men aren't and
Will never be like Edward or Jacob for that matter.
-I don't sparkle. I kiss like it was the last time,
I get angry when we part, it saddens me when you`re apart
I may start thinking things if I don't hear from you…
I'm about my business and my busyness
But making time for you is a must.
I think for myself, I know what I want
I know who I am, I know where I'm going

I can laugh at myself, I am comfortable with my sexuality
I am more than confident, impossible is but a word to me,
Love is but a word to me, family means everything
Culture are my roots, my past is my past but my
Present is a gift. I want to know more about you,
I love to hear your opinion, thoughts, idea
I feel your emotions I feed off your vibe,
I remain in awe of your beauty as a person
And as a dream, because I still am pinching myself
Wondering if your part of my reality.

-Netu-

The same. Always.

I will tell you exactly who I am and you either like it or you don't.
And to be quite frank with you it doesn't matter to me what
    others think of what I say.
But what does matter is that you understand that I am
    bewitched by you.
You are on my mind more often than you should be,
talking to you is a teaser, feeling you is never enough
kissing you should last forever. You're who I want, you're my
    woman
my lady and it kills me inside that this is what it is.
I want to know your name! I want to know what you're all about
I want to spend more time together
I want to take long walks, whatever
cuddle, kiss hug, pillow talk, time is time
and spent with you is always well spent!
you are my everything, my all and all, and if
these were my last words to you I would like you to read
each letter carefully because I did the same writing them for you.
My love, all is but dull without you,
I am… completely, most definitely, yours and yours alone
I long for you, I want you, and there is no one else
on my mind, there is no compatibility physically, intellectually
spiritually, emotionally, nothing. Nothing period that will
    match what we have.
you are half of me, you bring out the best in me,
I can stop but think that if this was my only chance to let you know
that there might be a chance that you wouldn't feel the same
because we both know love is out of our control.

regardless, I love you. I always have, and always will, the
    same. Always.

-Netu-

Patience for a Queen

It is now, more than ever, in my best interest to pass the time.
Because you know, good things take time.
According to the dictionary, patience is
The quality of endurance, under difficult circumstances,
in the face of delay or provocation.
Emotions may be fickle but
good-natured tolerance is always healthy.
It was at a point in my life arguable,
Because it is out of my nature to let things slide,
I make my destiny I don't wait for opportunities
I create them, but this, you, are out of my control.
Devine blessings are a gift, and I recognize that now more
    than ever.
You see, darling, I'm a go-getter,
I am the type to take the lead,
Get what I want. But I recon you're more than that,
And exhibiting forbearance
especially in my time of need
Displays my character,
Then I owe it to you- it is my duty to
Be patient because your
Invaluable,
My ever so precious
Queen.

-Netu-

Dangerously healthy

You're arguably and indisputably, the most infectious being
I've ever encountered in my life. Some kind of wonderful,
     some kind
Of irresistible blessing from sky. Who knows where you hide
     your wings,
Here's hoping you will find comfort in my heart,
My arms, safe away from all of the days stress, pressures and
     expectations.
You are more than words can explain, but here I am writing
     trying to explain
How devastatingly detrimental you are to my system and to
     my life.
I loose focus because of you,
I blush… I forget what I was thinking
I… smile much too often. You`re bad for me
You are dangerously healthy for me.
I enjoy every moment spent with you,
You and you alone,
No other can do what you do,
Make me feel the way you make me feel
Well spoken, well carried, everything you have,
But my kiss.

-Netu-

To whom it may concern- thank you

The use of words are an understatement to how I feel
That being said, at times it is the only way I can find to express
What it is that I feel.
You know its interesting because although we rarely
Communicate although we rarely touch or see each other,
I've never felt so close to someone.
Its as though I don't have to think, I don't have to try
To do- it just is, I just am, you just are and what we have is.
You see its hard to explain but I'm going to do my best to
Put it into words- you are absolutely splendid is what I'm saying.
I've been in love with you since the first day we met and its
       never been
The same. You are loveliness, beauty reincarnated
Whatever you would like to call it its real I see it
And I feel it. Not only in you but in myself
Baby, you bring out the best in me,
You make me a better man for myself,
And thus for others around me,
And most importantly for you.
Had I never met you, I wouldn't ever
Dream of being half the man I am today.
So for this,
I say

Thank you

-Netu-

Alphabetical love

Alphabetical love

All answers are always an inch away.
But be bold, be better, behold beauty in
Simplicity blindfolds.

Be courageous, carrying cunning, yet cautious
concepts of love. Carefully choose she who
Forfeits flaunting but acts in good gestures.
Gullible gentlemen halt at her feet,
Not knowing how she holds holism heavy hitting
indispensible, irreplaceable irresistible intellectual capacity.

It is irrefutable that imbedded in those jeans is much more than
Just lingerie. But you fools are just jesters, juveniles,
Killing kindness with knots of false pretences. Fake kings,
Your keys keep luring loveliness but like my last thought
Life moves on.

You'll find that her madness moans much
more than she does. Marks more memories not noticing
that the bare necessities of operations are openly
objectified by a vertical obsession. Open your minds
that part which peacefully passes past perspectives
which pull pre-planned pre-placed questions
Of quotes in respect to real reasons to tamper with time.

Thanks to that intangible feeling to unveil
unnecessary unbelievable unique views I keep
my love unconditional and my selection few
as others feast upon vast wooing.

One day my Walls will fall to the right one. Until then
I wait to see who has the will to want and the capability to
Xerox more than just xox's .

-Netu-

Speachless

If I could only spell your name with my body, then I would
    kiss you.
I would kiss you slowly, so passionately that you could hear
    me whisper
each letter, as our lips gently caress.

Call it chemistry, madness or insanity all of the above are true,
and all the above are real. True emotions which I feel for you,
hence whether I am madly in love or love you madly makes no
difference to me as both consist of some form of temporary
    madness
which I will never comprehend.

All that I know it`s that its real and that I feel it for you,
regardless of how you may see it, react, or believe it to be.
I remain unconditional, loyal, unchanged and unwilling to
    change
in respect to you.

That being said, here I am sharing my ``could'a should'a
    would'as``
writing down thoughts and emotions, when all that is to do,
is simply kiss.

-Netu-

Dear Lois

Kryptonite used to be a fictional element,
Mythos, originating from a broken society.
I used to feel like such an extraordinary being.
An ideal superior conceived by nothing less
Than dominance, power and creativity;

But when I met you, it all changed.
You taught me that no one prevails by virtue
Of being a ruthless egoist of superior strength.
Cunning force of will is only achieved through love.

At this time I felt like the clock is ticking,
And as minutes fly across the earth
Reality puts things in reverse and makes me wish for once,
That I could go back in time and avoid the worst.

Still fate leads the way.
And I must admit, although I regret losing you
Kryptonite never felt so good.
Although I might have gained back my lost powers,
Picked up my torn cape
I'll never forget you,
Because for the first time in my life,
Someone made me feel human.

-Netu-

Dessert or Disaster

I must confess,
I typically serve at the end of a meal,
Sweet food, good pastry, and fruits
but I guess there is a first time for everything.

30 minutes in and already two broken spatulas,
Four eggs thrown at a wall—all in passion- I assure you.
And as you look at the flour all over the kitchen floor,
My mind steams with thoughts of you watching on the side.

Soon you wont need to wonder when it is that
My drumming drum will numb your hum.
For most, to beat a drum is to gain a beat,
But for me its to enjoy your rhythm.
You never get the same results when you beat an egg.

That being said, here's what's on the menu:
You, pleased with yourself, watching me cook for you topless,
Little do you know that my retribution is a dish best served
        cold
And you wont need to taste it to know its sweet.

-Netu-

Name and digits please

Excuse me, can I talk to you for a minute?
you know, you look kind of familiar…
Looking as good as you want to be,
You those shoes and your ridiculously curvaceous hmm..
You're Just a product of loveliness

That's the way you make me feel.
In any event,
What's your name?

Mine's Netu… and I called you over to let you know
That I like your vibe, your walk,
your talk, and the way you dress
Your sweet aroma is forever engraved in my mind
And your footprints are imprints in my ear lobes.

You're all that and more, and whatever happens
by the end of this conversation,
I'd like your name, and your number.
I mean, if it's alright with you,
I know it might feel weird to
Contemplate whether or not to converse, let alone
walk away with a perfect stranger but…

There is no way to mistake love for foolishness
Because if I'm going to be a fool I will gladly
Be a fool for you. You know, one can never be too humble,

Anyway, I know you've had a busy day,
But I think it's times like these that you should
relax and let fate happen,
Let me handle things, give you a hand.
Perhaps you could even borrow my lips,
And I could spell out the first three digits:
613...

-Netu-

More than somebody to love

For you I'd write a symphony
With no use of violin, because sink or swim,
My voice would play it for you.
An instrumental passage a choral composition
expecting each note to pave a thousand miles
every key closer just to get to where you are.
Step to the beat of my heart, Strike repeatedly,
Shape and break old wounds and repeated blows.
Carve me into the man that I should be...

Make it new again,
Forget the ideal concept of love,
And what society thinks,
I see how they ruin our world with chick flicks,
Who needs them we could live ours.
I recon I am not the first one to give you all this attention
        But Baby listen...
I need more than just somebody to love I promise girl I swear
        Everyday I'd
bring the sun around,
I blow away the clouds. just to see you smile for me (Smile
        for me)

I would take, every second, Every single moment,
To cherish you, and make you realize
That before I met you all I had was a dream and a dime.

-Netu-

Yours to see

If beauty is in the eye of the beholder
then mine is forever yours to see; even with its imperfections,
I stand naked the way I am
present in my quality which wouldn't be fulfilled without
your intense pleasure or deep satisfaction.

To my mind,
whether arising from sensory
manifestations, a meaningful word or thought
I strive to remain in your eyes a personality
in which high emotional, physical, intellectual
and spiritual qualities make manifest.

-Netu-

I'll be ready

She Comes
Love is patient, love is kind.
Love is not jealous nor boastful;
It's not arrogant nor rude. Love does not insist on its own way.
It's not irritable or resentful; Love handles you at your worst,
To deserve you at your best.
Love is all things and perfect kindness. But above all,
Love is a practical joke.
A trick purposely made to make me mad.
I feel victimized. Its all Irony – But I do see the humor.
I wish God could send me an angel saying
"You've got Punked!"
I'm only human- lighthearted to a certain degree.
And although in some unpractical way, things work out,
this inherent divine strain of mockery presents itself much
    too often.
I wonder, can you not perceive how rude, how low the deed
    you do?
Karma plays on our generations' heart.
It pursues the purest taste of a satire, and back to me it comes.
love's plunder sends the gift they steel so sly;
And when the love I seemed to prize suddenly slips out of my
    grasp.
I can only watch as fate derives more thrills out of it,
what a marvelous adventure.
What was just a first impression
Gave me sleepless nights and disoriented thoughts.
Your always on my mind.
But I take it,
Because I know, when She comes,
I'll be ready.

-Netu-

Prenuptial agreement

It's no surprise to me that we are oblivious.
Most end up in divorce because they wait too
Long to find solutions or Rather, they don't solve them
    before tying the knot.
It's our independence that stands against humility.
If you`re in "love" there should be no fighting. False.
Chick flicks, brain washed out ideals
And now society's morals, ethics and values are shattered.
Instead of realizing that fighting can be healthy,
We just marry someone because we're in love.
What does that mean? That kind of love wears off.
So then, marry your best friend. No, but that is the basis of
    true love.
Because when that stage of hyperventilating
Hangs up at the other end of the phone,
Know that your perfect match's got assets in progress.
Words of Affirmation, Voicing how nice you look, or how
    great the dinner tasted.
Quality Time Some, believe that being together, doing things
    together and focusing in
On one another is the best way to show love.
Build something priceless. This is my love language.
What say you? Turn off the TV now and give us some
    undivided attention.
I mean, vanity is vanity all is vanity, but,
Gifts are universal in all cultures; She's heaven's gift to me.
And that's valuable, But understand that presents don't have
    to be expensive,
they just need to be meaningful to send a powerful message.

That's why before I say I do,
I will always remember her birthday, our anniversary,
She'll never feel neglected and unloved.
She's my creative spark,
And I want to marry her
Because I can't see myself without her
Not because its been a while that we've been together.
I'm ready for all of it, the best and the worst,
I understand that I'm with her for her, not just her qualities.
One day I'll be her man. And I'm sure because
Our love's defined by our ability
To understand every word we're NOT saying.

-Netu-

Pretty overrated part I

Pretty is overrated. It catches your attention,
But personality captures your heart. True beauty.
Then again, it's better to be beautiful than to be good,
but it is better to be good than to be ugly- right?
And understand that every time you forget to carry yourself,
You become uglier. Beauty refers the whole,
Not a daily does of set materialistic, self-gratifying ego.
You might be a pretty picture,
But your nothing without a frame.
When did we become such narcissists.
Our society's values were once used to denote vanity,
Now we conceit in egotism. Most of you are simply selfish!
But you know, you dress to impress. Applied
to a social situations, you men and women are the elite.
beautifully displaying an indifference to the plight of others.
Don't get me wrong, There is such thing as a reasonable
amount of healthy narcissism. But the media has created a
        dysfunctional materialistic epidemic.
It is useless for me to shout to you " Give me your hand !"
You don't know how to give. Instead you shout back:
" Take mine !" Power struggles, preoccupations with
possessions and gender confusion. This more than
anything else prevents us from living freely and nobly.
All these brand names are merely a symbol:
We want it not for ourselves, but because it will
content our spirit for the moment. Back to the pretty people,
Most of us seldom retain the same charm that you had when
        pursued.

-Netu-

Pretty overrated

Here's a tip:
Most men pursue pleasure with such breathless
haste, but hurry past it. You Search for " Mr. Right" without
knowing that its not "Mr. Right" your after.
The more you acquire, the more elusive options become.
Possessions are usually diminished by possession,
So understand that if you don't come down to earth
you too will be just another option.
But your complaints aren't over the lack of necessities,
They're indispensable – positive hindrances to
the elevation of my life. is not good to be too free.
Remember that next time your clubin'
It is not good to have everything,
I tip my hat to those who's pleasures are the cheapest.
Because they are beautiful people.

-Netu-

So be it

Talk not of wasted affection; affection never was wasted.
I know you are here, I feel you, so listen.
The art of finding love… is largely the art of persistence.
In seeking to discover the best in myself, I make destiny.
A mixture of admiration and humour, the surest recipes for
    affection.
The discovery of chemistry I do not understand.
But I know you'll be a sudden revelation,
and the kiss to follow, a discovery.
I do not direct the course of this journey,
The road to finding you is paved with lust. So be it.
I see past that.
I can demonstrate my emptiness
because I know that
True love comes to those who believe,
but never expect to find.

-Netu-

Reflection of a King

We've all desired affection to mend our broken hearts.
The type to leave footprint in our memories,
Even when disgraced with misfortune.
Sometime I find that we
Get so carried away with the pursuit of love
That we fail to see true beauty;
The realization of fate through
preparation and proper circumstances.
-caution expectations are most fatal.
we must come to love not by finding a perfect person,
but by learning to see an imperfect person perfectly.
Nevertheless there is beauty in simplicity,
But most of all
In friendship and she with whom you always laugh.

-Netu-

Fatal Attraction

I look, and I see
and I feel what is real
and its like I've seen this before, so I wait,
Hesitate, and contemplate
if you're worth my time, tears, my love,
or even my all
Your fragrance carried me too close.
So close that I can't help but stare, feel and then touch…
Girl your something else,
It's simple attraction, I just keep wanting and loving you
      more and more…
And as we kiss, I wait for the sky to open up
for this is how I know
you are what I've been waiting for.

-Netu-

My thoughts- you've got me

All you've got is me.
No car, no diamonds, no house, no company.
Just me.
My undivided, unconditional undying devotion.
And as these fools favour you with riches and silver tongues
I hope for you to discover in them the foolishness they conceal.
I am but a man, like any of them, but unlike them,
My true state of power and wealth is to be myself.
I have no riches but my thoughts.
and as long as they include you,
I'm wealthy.

-Netu-

Beauty Walks

She walks in beauty, like a sweet kill.
Heads snap back to watch her turn way.
I blame neither of those fools,
For if the price of looking be blindness,
I too will have a look.
Her eyes may pierce my soul,
and agitate my tender heart.
She, not even heaven could deny,
A ray of her splendour out values all that is luxury in the world.
Men softly lighten around her,
And even yet my body can't help but sweetly express
How I call for her caress,
So soft, so calm, yet eloquent,
She wins all that there is to offer . With her,
all seconds are well spent,
A mind at peace. For all below,
Is a man who's woman is priceless.

-Netu-

Patiently Impatient

I am not patient,
I will not be waiting,
Not passively that is.
I have much to gain, but so much more to lose.
So I'm not going anywhere.- Love doesn't have to be daring
    at all times.
Let nothing disturb fate,
Let nothing dismay time;
Take as much as you need because all things pass; But truth
    doesn't change.
If anything, I have discovered that the moments I have really
    lived,
are the moments spent with you.
Seeking yourself is but a developing philosophy,
a belief system that takes a lifetime.
You know who you are. But if you need time,
I'll be here to savour and enjoy both life's pains and pleasures.
Its obvious that you don't need to find me,
I'm right here,
not patient, not waiting,
Rather, my spirit bears with resignations, yes.
But above all, with serene belief that all is for you.

-Netu-

Love case

In the back of the bottom of the drawer of the dresser by my
     bed is a box.
In it you'll find a short letter.

It reads:

I was never one to want to read women,
but You make me wish I could.
I always want to go the extra mile to see you smile.
You make me want to open the door,
walk on the right side of the street,
be there when you`re shopping.
offer my jacket and wrap you in my arms.

We could cuddle, play fight, dance the night away,
or I could pin you on to the wall.
I trust you .
Its always real with you.
I know who you are, and with you
Its not always about sex. We could cuddle too,
hold each other, hug, caress, and just be.

In the back of the bottom of the drawer of the dresser by my
     bed is a box…
In it you'll find a short letter.

It reads: I love you

-Netu-

More than words

Imagine when I'll run my fingers through your hair
taste the sweetness of your neck
maybe nibble at your ear
and then whisper words like…
I Promise it`s more than that.

Your sweet body comes alive
the heat of our flesh touching
slowly undresses my fantasy.

I'll lay you down
While you welcome my caress
With your luscious lips and sexy curves
Imagine this the next time
I look into your eyes

-Netu-

Lust

In the still of my thoughts
Without time to intrude
I feel your presence
As fate's lips set upon
whispering soft and low
words that fill my mind with hope.

I can't help but feel aroused
The very moment the thought of you crosses me.
My thoughts may flick their flame
As I indulge and embrace the passion.

- But I hope it's more than that.

-Netu-

No intent

I never planned on falling in love but
you captured my heart and stirred my soul.
- I guess sometimes fate just
fills the air with chemistry.

I can't help but feel aroused
The very moment you come near
I indulge and embrace the passion.

My thoughts may flick their flame
and at times drive me insane.
But silence is always comfortable
When our eyes meet.

-Netu-

X marks the spot

If you wonder where X marks the spot,
You've embarked on a hunt to find your treasure.
Precious seekers, the following should direct you in your quest:
Poor self expression is a reflection of poor self image.
Becoming the unique individual you're looking for
Is all about expressing your individuality.
Love does not care to define. It is never in a hurry to do so.
So just be you. And not only will you stand out,
but you'll have forgotten that fate brings you closer
to your ever so precious…
Life's romance is to be pleasantly surprised.
Be patient. Life doesn't normally work on your schedule.
Its rarely early,
Never late, but always on time.
Let your experiences color your world.
But don't rush time, irrational expectations can ruin any
        potential.
And contrary to popular belief,
"happily ever after." Is not a cash back guarantee.
You get what you put in.
So be ready, and willing to compromise.
don't go looking , it's where you least expect it to be.
It's so easy to fall but hard to find someone who will catch you.
So for now, you look out for yourself,
it will be alright. Fate will work it out.

-Netu-

How dare you

How dare you walk into my life,
Cause confusion in my world and with a wink and a smile
Seize complete power.
You weakened my wall by holding my hand;
By being the woman that I love
And showing me care in just one kiss.

How dare you walk into my life unannounced;
Leaving me dreaming of every moment
we've spent together and thinking of every ounce
Of desire I feel to have our souls connect in such passion
-it's surreal;

To feel your heart pounding against my chest,
To be entangled in each other's arms,
My lips kissing yours…
Eyes exploring the depth of my being

How dare you walk into my life and expose these thoughts that
I have buried for so long,
That I have been able to suppress
So that I may go on;

You've put me in a spot from which I cannot move,
You've made me vulnerable again,
How dare you do this to me.

-Netu-

How it blooms

I was never truly in love until
I understood every word you weren't saying
What it meant to be natural,
No effort required.
Although nothing worth fighting for is
ever as simple as it may appear,
True love is found in the most
Awkward situations. and as I
Leave procrastination and all of
It down the line. Know that
Efforts will reap
Much more than just what
I believe to be the perfect
Reality. I find it
Absolutely ironic that I
Now am in this
Disposition, life is blooming,
And as what we feel flourishes,
Understand what I didn't say.

-Netu-

First and foremost

Patience, kindness.
No envy, boasts, nor pride.
No rudeness, but selflessness.
I will be calm and collected;
not easily angered, keep no record of wrongs.
I won't delight in faults but rejoice in integrity
and unconditional love. I will always protect,
always trust, always persevere. I won't fail you.
And where there are prophecies, I will cease;
where there are tongues, I will be still.

Now of all the above three remain: faith, hope and love.
But the greatest of these is the promise that I do,
and I will always love. Love was
but an empty vessel carried
four letters until you gave it meaning...
Love was but a thought given to me
By the media, and society...
Love was easy, love was supposed to be,
love was magic. But the truth is...
love is hard, love is work, love is compromise
and first and foremost...
love is a choice.

-Netu-

Kiss & Cuddle

I won't forget to kiss and cuddle,
hug and give you massages or scratch your head.
I will cherish you and treat you like the woman you are.
I will always go the extra mile to see you smile.
I'll never forget to say those four letter words,
just because its nice for you to hear them.
And I vow to get a little jealous at times.
I promise to do my best to make you feel safe
and comfortable in intimate moments.
I'll always let you know that I think you're hot.
I'll tell you you're beautiful. Because you are.
I will do my best to notice the effort you make for me.
I will be consistent- but never predictable.
I will be engaged physically and mentally;
listen when you talk or vent. Connect with and pay attention
-Especially to the little things. Most of all,
I promise to be bubbly and humble.
I won't take everything too seriously
I will be dedicated and devoted.
I am not perfect, but I will strive to be in
my imperfections the man of your dreams.

-Netu-

The truth hurts

You hurt me,
Emotionally,
Physically,
You who I trusted with no doubt in the world;
who I spared my time for,
shared my most intimate thoughts
even you let me down.
Although you had no intentions for it,
life to turn out the way it did.

I realized: ultimately it is a choice;
Should you truly want to be with me, you'll act.
Contrary to popular belief,
my heart's scattered on the floor;
with nothing left to give.
the only person to piece me back together,
Is me.

-Netu-

Day dreaming

Everything feels right when
We're laying in my room,
beside each other in silence.
My arms wrapped around you,
Looking at the ceiling
You kiss me sweet and softly,
I feel your warm gentle touch,
As your presence frees my protected
thoughts.

There is beauty in imperfection, hence
My world before me is perfect.
There's nowhere else I want to be,
Hand in hand, you and me.

You swept me off my feet,
Nothing could be more right,
than what you've done to me.

-Netu-

Jeopardy

For a moment in time, my life was Jeopardy
Featuring trivia in topics including lust, selflessness
true love and how history tends to always repeats itself.

Through dates, I was exposed to
a unique answer-and-question
experience in which I; the contestant
was presented with clues in the form of answers,
and had to respond in question form.
-it was one of the most Memorable Episodes of my life.

At times I waited for destiny's` touch to help pick my choices,
turning maybes into yes's or nos
but waiting only tweaked my mind
and weakened my decision,

Hence why now I prefer my life handpicked by fate.
Excuses are many, and reasons all vary
but the time was up,
And answer was as follows:

Answer: unconditional love
Response: you.

-Netu-

See-through

What of gender roles?….
morals, ethics,
principles, culture and values too…

See right through,
ignore my disguise and facades ,
because truth be told,
you and I are one in the same
see right through.

- I feel stupid
but at least I know I'm telling you the truth..
I'm insecure…
But there are certain things I need to hear
from your lips…

But are you willing to drop your fears…
drop your pride…
and pick up your broken pieces…
stick it out and hold my hand?

Are you willing to let me give you
everything you deserve and in return
be mine?…

- if not….
what are we doing?

-Netu-

Intellectually celibate

If I have sex with you
leave come and arrive with you,
does that give me the right to hold your hand,
kiss you in public and say " boo" ?

Truth be told I'm tired of feeling like a fool,
being treated like a foreigner…
Trust me I have needs but maybe
When you're here today and gone today,
the ends don't justify the means…

I need your everything…
I want to know you're mine
and I have nothing to worry about
I want to be insecure… – Damn it!
I want to be vulnerable… and feel safe too.

I want to give you my all and know
that you want to take advantage of it.
truth be told nice guys finish last and you know it…

So what of me?
I`m trapped between who I am,
who I'll be and who I can be
and still sex is the same.

-Netu-

Divine cliche

My eyes follow your curves,
and I don't know what it is
But the way your hips sway
tags what my mind can't fathom
The overflowing of the heart, I guess.

It`s as though words come out with their own intentions
passed that of small talk or superficial conversation
But should silence settle
A smile and a giggle is all it takes…

I believe fate will lead us to each other
as we both discover
that this was never goodbye
It was simply " I'll see you later."

-Netu-

Words are not enough

It's hard to describe, in just a few paragraphs,
a friendship that grew over the course
of time through which a simple acquaintance
turned into my best friend.

In spite of our differences, and there were many,
we became almost inseparable.
Rarely a day went by, and never a week,
without spending intensive amounts of time together.

Doing things that best friends do.
"I miss you" can not display
The depths of how I care.
At this point words betray
The extent of what I dare not to say.

Not even "I need you"
can convey the extent of my desire.
The words "I love you" do not portray
The heights of my friendship.

-Netu-

To my best friend

I know you'll never forget. And although you've forgiven,
I need your friendship More than you'll ever know.

I miss your calls
Our endless talks
and long walks to only places we would go

Although I can't even bear to look at you anymore,
a mistake is a mistake. A perfect example of how
one night, and a few thoughtless actions,
Make emotions irreversible.

As much as we would like to
I can not forget
And start all over.

If time is what you need,
Then that's what you'll get.

Who knows if we'll meet again,
But I want you to know,
You're my best friend.

-Netu-

Unselfishly selfish

Be expressive without saying a word…
know true communication in what's unsaid…
hold me down…
cherish, caress and be my lover…
Only mine…

call.. text.. whatever…
think of me as often as I think of you…
move strategically… think critically and act selflessly…
but where I'm concerned selfishly…
Take my love and appreciate it…
Understand that you satisfy me by being satisfied…
Consider my feelings…
as selfish as they may be…

Drive me madly in love,
And be proud of yourself.
Know who you are.
Don't be afraid to touch, kiss, play…
But no mind games –

find a reason… to get closer
Its never too late or too early
you could get to me whenever you'd like…
and still laugh…

You are rare in your kind… but always good to find.
and when fate does gives me way…
I probably won't notice that your standing right in front of
    me…

-Netu-

She's my fantasy

A good woman is hard to find, but a hard woman is good to
    find.
Words that are engraved in my mind as her touch reflects her
    personality…

She lives through me as I through her and
takes me as I am, regardless of my faults,
Enjoys comfortable silence and lives in the little moments
- yet frowns by kissing, gets mad by hugging ,
gripping hard and forgives me in the blink of an eye.

She has higher expectations for herself than I for her,
She gets jealous at the mention of another,
And is the first to kiss me goodnight, and whisper good
    morning
"She" is beauty, deeper than the eyes can see…

My soul food cooking, ridiculously curvaceous Queen
She does not judge me, but gets upset at my actions
She stands by my side and is proud to be my lady
She confides in me, shares the memories and the moments
as they come and go.

She's honest, loyal, humble and oh so kind…
an astonishing intellectual, She who's mind flows
like rhythm and moves only as fast as She needs to…
She who will take my hand without hesitation…
Be soft, tender, smooth and ever so precious…
She's my fantasy.

-Netu-

Walk and talk

Let`s meet face to face , just me and you
go for a long walk and talk endlessly,
stimulate each other intellectually,
Because morals, values and ethics should be just as
important as a nice behind, sweet lips and a pretty face.

I've recognized that you're definitely not a typical "chick",
Because as we take the time to get to know each other
I find that you naturally bring out the best in me.
But you don't have to take my word for it.-Actions speak
     louder.

Sooner or later, I'll kiss you and stand right here…
because you deserve more than just being left wondering:
"where is he going?"

-Netu-

First date

Charm was a result of a quick glance,
and maybe three seconds, when we first met.
Your smile formed a nearly irreversible
encounter for it set the tone for all that was to follow.
This was beyond me. I've read body language before,
but none like yours, putting a great deal of emphasis
on the little things...

We had just met each other,
yet all was natural between us...
Not even a movie script could have created such a scene.
In fact, it worked out too well.
And as any gentleman would do, I kissed you.

We sat there and let small talk entertain us...
and before I knew it, reality hit
it was time for you to go...
My eyes lingered at your hips swaying away...
And your smile saying " Bye for now."
The "take-charge" gentleman got swept off his feet.

- but all you did was kiss me...

-Netu-

"B"

I missed you on the road somewhere
Between life and four letters.
Now I sit back, observe and question
whether pride and determination are strong enough
to fuel hope for fate's course not to swerve.

Time continues and the world contains us both,
but while you elude, must I pursue?
-It seems too much like fate for me not to.
But what if I fail of my purpose here?
Should I dry my eyes and laugh at the fall,
or get up to begin again?
-The chase takes up my mind that's all.

We've changed and we're finding our own place in life,
But I know that when a tear drops
or a smile spreads across your face,
we'll come to each other because no matter where this crazy
world takes us, true friendship remains.

-Netu-

Things we do

There can be no happiness if the things we believe
in are different from the things we do. Hence, I write:

I look back on our moments
and appreciate how far we've come
For the vision that we've set in our minds,
the ideal that we've enthroned in our hearts,
this we will build our life by,
and this we will become.

As we pave memory lane,
every step leaving the finest of foot prints
We become the strongest.
Not because we are protected from the storm
But rather because we are the ones that stand in the open
compelled to struggle for our existence .

Through all these many years;
The thought of a woman whose most gentle soul,
Embraces me each day …
A woman whom I care for
Much more than words can say.

-Netu-

A beautiful woman part I

Always consider a beautiful woman;
One who with a light touch of words,
May have your mind lingering
in the softest of ways.
A real woman, not seen often enough,
sincerely a creature that would add
immeasurable peace of mind.
As she walks, all that 's left of her are thoughts
hoping to meet in her aspect all that's tender.
I care only to express how she dwells in-place.
So soft, so calm, yet eloquent,
She is truly a heart whose nature is divine.
Her curves sway the mind, but it is
Her mind that molds and makes.
Stimulating thoughts and flow that so easily
Take my breath away.

-Netu-

About the Author...

Emmanuel Udinetu-Kuonso Kahumbu (born November 7, 1989) is an artist under the mononym Netu. He is most recognized for his charisma, subtle sensuality and his way with words charisma. He personalizes his approach to writing by imprinting his romantic and passionate signature into all his works. A charismatic fusion of class and elegance, with a rugged sexy twist. His delivery and personality make his works of art exciting and impactful . This first publication of his works has made his name known to all romantics at heart. He is recognised for his beautifully touching and pure tales. Although love is a different thing for most of us, he believes these poems are universal and will mean something to each of us. This is one of the best ways that he knows to inspire, open minds and bottle common sense.